P9-CQI-788

A Note to Parents and Teachers

Kids can imagine, kids can laugh and kids can learn to read with this exciting new series of first readers. Each book in the Kids Can Read series has been especially written, illustrated and designed for beginning readers. Humorous, easy-to-read stories, appealing characters, and engaging illustrations make for books that kids will want to read over and over again.

To make selecting a book easy for kids, parents and teachers, the Kids Can Read series offers three levels based on different reading abilities:

Level 1: Kids Can Start to Read

Short stories, simple sentences, easy vocabulary, lots of repetition and visual clues for kids just beginning to read.

Level 2: Kids Can Read with Help

Longer stories, varied sentences, increased vocabulary, some repetition and visual clues for kids who have some reading skills, but may need a little help.

Level 3: Kids Can Read Alone

Longer, more complex stories and sentences, more challenging vocabulary, language play, minimal repetition and visual clues for kids who are reading by themselves.

With the Kids Can Read series, kids can enter a new and exciting world of reading!

Funtime Riddles

Marilyn Helmer

Jane Kurisu

Kids Can Press

What game do bakers play on their lunch break?

Tic Tac Dough

How is a baseball game like a cake?

They both need a good batter.

Why did the children cross the playground?

To get to the other slide

How did the bowler fix the hole in his pants?

With bowling pins

What would you get if you crossed two elephants with a whale?

A huge pair of swimming trunks!

Why is it no fun to play soccer with pigs?

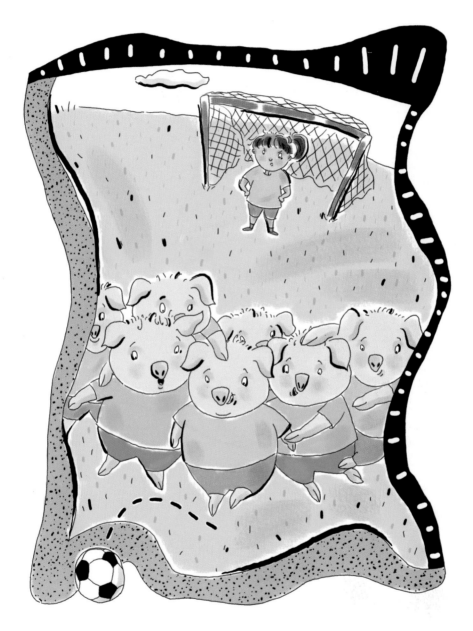

Because they always hog the ball

What kind of bird hangs around ski resorts?

A ski-gull

Why don't cheetahs like to play hide and seek?

Because they're always spotted

What kind of boat does a prize-winning athlete sail on?

A champion-ship

What do little mice do for fun in the winter?

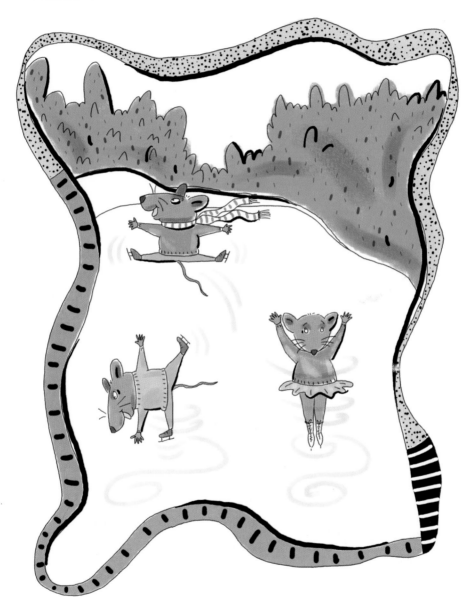

They go mice-skating.

11

Why couldn't the sailors play cards on the boat?

Because the captain was standing on the deck

What is a ghost's favorite board game?

Moan-opoly

Why was the hockey player covered with spots?

Because she had chicken pucks

Why do golfers always carry an extra pair
of socks?

In case they get a hole-in-one

What game do mama birds play with their baby birds?

Beak-a-boo

Where do tigers get their exercise?

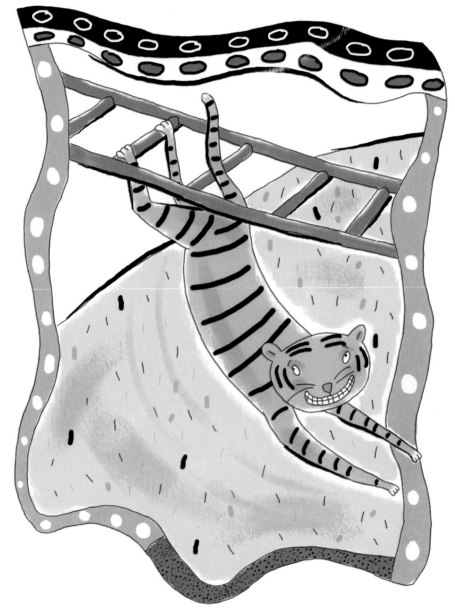

On jungle gyms

What kind of underwear does a prizefighter wear?

Boxer shorts

Why didn't the rooster want to go bungee jumping?

He was too chicken.

How did the hot dog do in the race?

He was the wiener!

What sidewalk game do rabbits always win?

Hopscotch

Why are fish such bad tennis players?

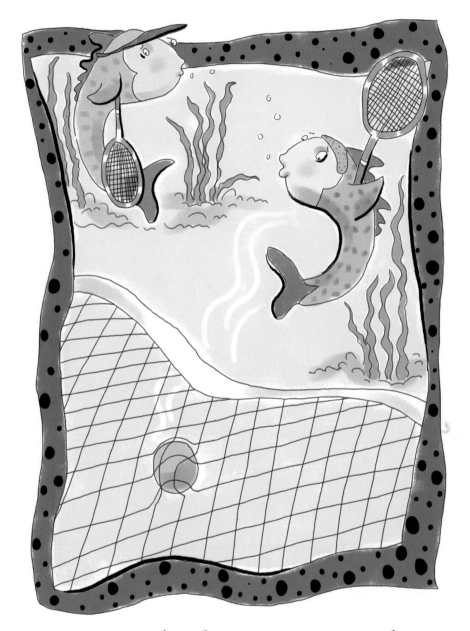

They don't want to get near the net.

Why was the baseball player sent to jail?

He was caught stealing bases.

What kind of fish is easiest to catch at night?

A starfish

Why are football stadiums always cool?

Because the seats are filled with fans

What do frogs like to play at bedtime?

Sleep-frog

How did the rower stop her boat?

She whoa, whoa, whoa-ed the boat.

What game do pigs like best?

Pig-pong

Why are basketball courts usually wet?

Because the players dribble all over them

What did one tuna say to the other when they were playing cards?

Go fish!

Why did the girl wear Rollerblades when she sat in the rocking chair?

Because she wanted to rock and roll

For my son, Christopher, who is a sports and games guy — M.H.
For David and Celine — J.K.

Kids Can Read is a trademark of Kids Can Press

Kids Can Press acknowledges the financial support of the Government of Ontario, through the Ontario Media Development Corporation's Ontario Book Initiative; the Ontario Arts Council; the Canada Council for the Arts; and the Government of Canada, through the BPIDP, for our publishing activity.

Published in Canada by
Kids Can Press Ltd.
29 Birch Avenue
Toronto, ON M4V 1E2

Published in the U.S. by
Kids Can Press Ltd.
2250 Military Road
Tonawanda, NY 14150

www.kidscanpress.com

Edited by David MacDonald
Designed by Marie Bartholomew
Printed in Hong Kong, China, by Wing King Tong

The hardcover edition of this book is smyth sewn casebound.
The paperback edition of this book is limp sewn with a drawn-on cover.

CM 04 0 9 8 7 6 5 4 3 2 1
CM PA 04 0 9 8 7 6 5 4 3 2 1

National Library of Canada Cataloguing in Publication Data

Helmer, Marilyn
        Funtime riddles / Marilyn Helmer, Jane Kurisu.

(Kids Can read)
ISBN 1-55337-579-3 (bound).   ISBN 1-55337-580-7 (pbk.)

1. Riddles, Juvenile. I. Kurisu, Jane II. Title. III. Series: Kids Can read (Toronto, Ont.)

PN6371.5.H443 2004   jC818'.5402   C2003-902328-1

Kids Can Press is a **corus™** Entertainment company